I0480497

Abstract

In India, Dr. B. R. Ambedkar (1891-1956), the Chief Architect of the Indian Constitution who led from the front one of the biggest human rights struggles of the oppressed in the world. In four decades (1916-1956) of his intellectual, socio-political public life he was almost part and parcel of almost all national developments, shaping the destiny of new born Indian republic on modern values of liberal democracy. Yet, for various socio-political reasons his multifaceted yeoman services remain unknown to the world. However, in India, day by day Dr B. R. Ambedkar's legacy thrives in an intriguing intellectual and political milieu. His life struggle, movement and enormous scholastic English writings on subjects of national importance has attracted the attention of enlightened world in liberating movements of the subjugated. Therefore, there is an absolute need to know the fundamentals of Ambedkarism through "Dynamics & Relvance of Ambedkarism."

Key Words

Ambedkar-Buddhism-Constitution-Historiography-Dynamisim-Ambedkarism- Ideology- Constitutionalism-Development-Governance-Labour-cultural.

1

DYNAMICS AND RELEVANCE OF AMBEDKARISM

Introduction

With growing relevance of Dr. Ambedkar's thoughts, struggle as well as his socio-political space in Indian politics, in recent past everybody is interested in studying Ambedkar, be it the centrists, leftists and even right wing forces. It is welcome move. All of those who once opposed him by all possible means are now looking at him afresh, evaluating his multi-faceted thoughts and contributions. In fact there is a strange race to appropriate his legacy, writings, thoughts and struggle. How and why this miracle, is the first and foremost step to commence any discourse on Dr. Ambedkar.

The man who was once upon a time ridiculed by his opponents with diatribe, such as, 'a British stooge', 'opponent of M. K. Gandhi', 'a conformist Hindu', 'a destroyer of the Hindu religion', 'merely a leader of untouchables', 'unpatriotic', 'the man who left behind a dual and sometimes confusing legacy', has turned into a Bharat Ratna, Chief Architect of the Indian Constitution thus occupying a space in the list of builders of modern India. And strikingly, also finds a place in the morning prayer of

RSS-a Hindu fascist organisation to which Dr. Ambedkar always condemned.

This change in the outlook of all these anti-Ambedkar forces is a product of time and victory of an ideology and struggle of Dr. Ambedkar-which day by day is occupying a new social constituencies, not only in India but globally at large. His thoughts and struggle both are becoming more and more relevant in liberation struggles of downtroddens and oppressed. The modern so called upholders of Ambedkar's ideology, methods and his struggle- the leftists, rightists, centrists and even naxalites, for their own selfish motives, caste-class bias, all have been guilty of Ambedkar's annihilation-the very author of "Annihilation of Caste." Their acceptance to Ambedkarism is not their choice but an effect of their failure to succeed in their endeavours-a part of a politics of accommodation. From RSS leaders to Gandhian, leftists scholars and even market scholars like Arun Shourie, all have tried through their diatribe to destabilize Ambedkar's solitary place in the modern Indian history.

I fully agree that nobody holds patent rights for articulation and propagation of Ambedkarism and every great man who have changed the course of human history, including Dr. Ambedkar, all are subject to exploration by each man, generation in different conditions. Ultimately what man thinks is a sociological fact. Therefore, every man in the world is free to undertake Ambedkar's assessment and reassessment in his own way. As a consequence, there is no dearth of scholars who by their efforts are trying to define, redefine Dr. Ambedkar. However, while doing so, barring some genuine and exceptional efforts, the forces who once worked for his extermination from the socio-political landscape of India, or in a part of larger conspiracy to silence Ambedkar who have taken complete care to limit him only to untouchables, even while subscribing to Ambedkarism due to their socio-political compulsion, are not completely divorcing their dishonesty, a hereditary character in their DNA.

So now, after the stages of approbation and appropriation of Dr. Ambedkar, they have devised a new method of polluting and infecting Ambedkarism with their own rejected and discarded doctrines in the name of critical enquiry of Ambedkarism, testing his vision in the changed scenario, the need to recover 'the real Ambedkar', unlocking Ambedkarism or situating him in the expanded horizons of emancipatory politics at global level with all kinds of tall claims of wisdom and what not.

In this process, on one side, systematic attempts are made to install distorted Ambedkar in so far unoccupied socio-political territories, to build up another wall of opinion but on the other side simultaneous efforts are also being made to weaken or demolish the basic tenets of Ambedkarism. The strategic method is very simple. On one hand you eulogise distorted Ambedkar to make an inroad for mass acceptability but inject his radical discourse with your rejected and discarded ideas, ism, etc., by pinpointing some contrasts and contradictions in Ambedkarism to ignorant classes or charging Dr. Ambedkar himself with inconsistencies in his thoughts and actions. And there lies the real danger.

In such an exercise, with extreme cunningness, attempts are made to reduce Dr. Ambedkar to a only mini-reformist figure. Here attempts are made to destroy Dr. Ambedkar by using Ambedkar, by exhibiting contrasts and contradictions in his struggle and thoughts, very often by quoting him out of context. For example, Dr. Ambedkar's statement in the Rajya Sabha on September 2, 1953, in the debate on Andhra State Bill 1953. Participating in the debate, in an angry outburst he said, "Sir, my friends tell me that I have made the Constitution. But I am quite prepared to say that I shall be first person to burn it out." Definitely, in a plane manner this statement is in contrast to his established position of principle authorship of the Indian Constitution.

But Dr. Ambedkar's subsequent explanation to his statement is conveniently forgotten or ignored. On March 19, 1955, participating in a debate on Constitution (Fourth) Amendment Bill, 1954, and on being reminded by another member Dr. Anup Singh, of his earlier statement of burning the constitution, he said, "My friends says that the last time when I spoke, I said that I wanted to burn the Constitution. Well in a hurry I did not explain the reason. Now that my friend has given me the opportunity, I think I shall give the reason. The reason is this: We built a temple for a god to come in and reside, but before the god could be installed, if the devil had taken possession of it, what else could we do except destroy the temple? We did not intend that it should be occupied by the Asuras (demons) . We intended it to be occupied by the devas (gods) that is the reason why I said I would rather like to burn it."

The game plan is very simple. You destroy Dr. Ambedkar's equation with constitutionalism and thereby open a gate for unconstitutional methods-anarchical revolutionary ways which have been out rightly discarded by Dr. Ambedkar-calling it as a "grammar of anarchy."

Thus, Ambedkarite ideology and struggle in a comprehensive manner is a problematic challenge to all those who are not votaries of democratic revolution or constitutional transformation. For them Ambedkar's constitutionalism is an obstacle in their march and as long as it persists, it is impossible for them to have their final say.

Dr. Ambedkar not only opposed the brahmanical hegemony, but he had the courage and conviction of unparallel level to disregard Gandhians philosophy of Indian villages, the concept of trusteeship and the Swaraj which no Indian intellectual or a political leader has been able to do so far. Equally he was quite vocal in his opposition to Hindu nationalists and their ideology. And certainly he was not in favour of communists and in no way to any kinds of blood-shed revolutionary methods. In spite of this huge army of opponents, Dr. Ambedkar's emergence as a source of inspiration, an idealistic position to teeming millions and millions, poor deprived masses is unique in history. No other person than Dr. Ambedkar is able to rule the hearts and minds of millions and millions, even after 64 years of his demise. Therefore, the people who have been left with no option of either accepting or rejecting Ambedkar are constantly in search of new devices, methods so that they can sell their little products in the brand name of Dr. Ambedkar.

In this scenario, there is an absolute need to know the fundamentals of Ambedkarism. The present monograph is aimed with this necessity. Of course, at the outset it needs to be admitted that, the man who was extraordinarily active in socio-political life of India for four decades (1916-1956), who was actively involved in all the constitutional developments in India, (from 1919 to 1950), the member of Bombay Legislative Assembly for near about 13 years, in the Viceroy's Executive Council as the In-charge Minister of Labour, Water Management and Power Generation from 1942 to 1946, from 1946 to 1950 the Chief Architect of the Indian Constitution, from 1947 to 1951 the first Law Minister of independent India, the strongest dissenting voice in the Indian parliament from 1952 till death, along with his vast treasure of seminal writings on his credit, the organiser, mobilise of poor stratified downtrodden mass culminating them into one of the biggest human rights movement in the globe by peaceful and democratic means and logically ending it into the cultural revolution of Buddhism in 1956, besides several other laurels to his credit, could not be confined and explained in few pages of monograph.   Yet, the monograph is authored in the hope that it also has something to offer you. I sincerely hope that this write-up will be enough to generate the interest in readers to know more about Dr. Ambedkar and his struggle.

Dr. B. R. Ambedkar, famously revered as Dr. Babasaheb Ambedkar one of the greatest sons of India dedicated his entire life for building up, brick by brick one of the greatest human rights struggles in the world to secure the dignity to oppressed and suppressed for centuries. His excellence in the field of knowledge was well acknowledged by the world leading educational centers, such as, London School of Economics, Columbia University of USA, but except

Usmania- the only Indian University, no other university has discovered the towering intelligence and wisdom in him.

From Anthropology to Constitutional law and from Indian historiography to Economics, his vast reservoir of knowledge has accorded a new insight into such areas of knowledge. He is the one who commenced his journey from Bahishkrit Hitkarini Sabha to revival and redefining Buddhism, and thereby changed the social-cultural landscape of India. His sincerity, courage and determination was always beyond the manageable capacity of the so-called nationalist, social as well as political forces and therefore stood against all odds and his powerful opponents. From problems of small land holdings in India to how should India's foreign affairs be conducted by the governments in the country in the changing world scenario, he has offered a lot. From India's partition to unified strong independent sovereign nation, he was the one who by his distinct approach dominated the mainstream politics of India for near about two and half decade, i.e. from 1930 to 1955.

Yet, in India, the centres of learning, universities and governmental funded so-called autonomous research bodies, calling themselves the knowledge industries of India find either no space or very little space, in curricula or research on Dr. Ambedkar, almost complete annihilation of the very author of "Annihilation of caste". "The Indian social science landscape has disarticulated Babasaheb Ambedkar by studious theoretical silence....In any case, the communities of knowledge and communities of powering India are united in their marginalization of Babasaheb. Neither politics nor knowledge, discovers in him a vision towards which India may move. Is this due to the possibility that practices of power and of knowledge in India are incoherent before a heretical discourse, especially when it emanates from an untouchable"[1].

Generally, in India, traditionally social reformers are remembered, respected and revered, but Ambedkar's crime was that he was not merely a social reformer but more than that. He ruthlessly attacked the monolithic caste structure, its lawless laws and articulated militant power discourse among millions of his followers arousing them to revolt and overthrow the status-quoist power structure by becoming the governing class to rule this land. Among all social reformers and leaders of modern India, perhaps, Dr. Ambedkar was the only exceptional one who strived for ending the oppressor's rule and replacing it with the rule of powerless people.

However, since 1991, Dr. Ambedkar's Birth Centenary Year, there has been a sea change. Today, barring few, even Ambedkar's diehard critics spare no words in idolizing him. Gandhi and Nehru's Congress party, the Indian Communists who hand in glove with the Congress party had worked together to outlaw him from Indian politics in the very first general election of 1951-52, have been forced adopt Dr. Ambedkar as one of their heroes. The RSS and Bhartiya Janata Party-so-called Hindu nationalist organizations co-opted Ambedkar among a galaxy of historic Hindu models. From old conservative Gandhians to the new creed of Naxalites, everyone, desire and require, Dr. Ambedkar to sustain themselves. According to some of his diehard critics like Arun Shourie, Ambedkar has become an idol and is worshipped like a god[2,] although he was not only the non-believer of gods but destroyer of idols.

The new glorification of Babasaheb Ambedkar, however, has further complicated the task of understanding Dr. Ambedkar. Due to the adoption of Ambedkar by all forces, leftist, rightists, centrists and even all those who are neither here nor there understanding Dr. Ambedkar in its correct perspective has become difficult. Because, Dr. Ambedkar is represented by each one of them, conveniently, according to their need, understanding making the innocent mass, followers of Babasaheb to be their captive audience, supporters and voters to keep intact the same power structure which Ambedkar wanted to demolish. But at the same time I must also mention that the same illiterate, emotional, and even unorganised mass if come across any intentional attacks either on Ambedkar's statue or ideology, they retaliate with any means including their life[3]. But in the recent past, the Ambedkar festivals, celebrations and absorption by vested interests for their self protections and articulations have completely diluted and killed the spirit and identity of Ambedkarism. As a consequence, even today, Dr. Ambedkar remains less understood and more misunderstood to large Indians.

There have been many 'ism's in India, such as, Brahmanism, Hinduism, Sikhism, Buddhism, Gandhism, Marxism, Socialism, Communism, etc. The title of this monograph "Dynamics and Relevance of Ambedkarism" will make you to think about one more 'ism', that is Ambedkarism. Indeed, it is a great difficulty to deduce the principles of Ambedkarism because Dr. Ambedkar was never engaged in the formulation of theory of human liberation but was practically engaged in leading one of the biggest human rights struggle from the front, facing several odds.

Dr. Ambedkar's revolt, Ambedkarism, is the reconstructive ideology with an agenda of annihilation of caste, in sequel to the struggles of Charvaka, Buddha, Mahatma Phuley, Kabir and others all those, who revolted against the culture of casteism, untouchability and oppression. In some of the matters, Dr. Ambedkar has dealt it independently. Dr. Ambedkar's canvass of activity was so vast and multi-dimensional that, it becomes difficult for any scholar to grasp him in its entirety. He has struggled, written and spoken so much on divergent subjects and changing contexts that naturally tempts any scholar to level a charge of inconsistency.

Therefore, Ambedkarism is construed as a body of collective thoughts and actions of Dr. Ambedkar on various issues-from economics to politics, from separate settlements of untouchables to the call to untouchables to capture the political power, from merely independence from the foreign yoke to social democracy. In essence, it is the liberation ideology for the victims of caste culture by peaceful, constitutional means and aimed with reconstruction of the Indian caste-ridden society on the pillars of liberty, equality, fraternity and justice to all, like his great Masters (Gurus) – Lord Buddha, Mahatma Phuley and saint Kabir.[4]

During his long struggle from 1916 to 1956, in four decades, he has spoken, and written on various themes in volumes and volumes, undertook several human rights struggles, represented several bodies in India and abroad and was the prominent force in independent India's constitution making process, adopted sometime strategies of conflict and reconciliation which have left many confused. This has led on him the charge of inconsistency. But Dr. Babasaheb, undeterred by such criticism countered by saying that, 'consistency is virtue of an ass'. Therefore, to construe 'Ambedkarism' in its totality is a gigantic task and hence this writing is confined to some of the neglected but significant aspects of 'Ambedkarism' which will on one hand render the necessary assistance to the critics of Dr. Ambedkar and on the other hand will provide an analytical understanding of Ambedkar's thoughts, its dynamism and relevance to 'genuine Ambedkarites' activists as well as scholars –certainly not to enlighten stooge (*Chamcha)* Ambedkarites[5].

For some ignorant critics, Ambedkarism it is an 'ideology in which mediocrity is the norm, vulgarity is the right, in which standards are an elitist conspiracy, in which civility and reason are the veneer of the well-to-do, in which intimidation is argument, and assault is proof. Among the liberals this ideology has become the rationalization for capitulation. And among the leaders of so-called Dalits and OBCs, and of the Muslims it has become the justification for 'direct action"[6]. Whether somebody likes it or not, approves or disapproves, today *'Ambedkarism'*- ideology and struggle, both are a living force.

In 21st century, despite Dr. Ambedkar yeoman services in nation building, unfortunately, Dr. Ambedkar is projected as synonymous to *Dalits* and reservation policy to a common non-dalit mass. With class interest, public opinion mechanisms in the country and anti *Ambedkarite* forces are never tired in making such propaganda so as to limit Ambedkar's constituency. But now day by day, Ambedkar's yeoman services to the nation are coming at the forefront. Having said so, in the following 12 significant points let us try to understand the basic tenets of Ambedkarim.

1. Dr. Ambedkar's Model of Development.

Dr. Ambedkar was an economist of par excellence. At the age of 24, in 1913-1915, he authored the "Ancient Indian Commerce" which was a subject of dissertation in fulfillment of the requirement of M.A. examination of Columbia University, which later on he changed to "Administration and Finance of the East Indian Company and obtained his M.A. degree in Economics from Columbia University, USA. In 1916 he was awarded with Ph. D. degree for his thesis, "The Evolution of Provincial Finance in British India" by the same university. In 1918 his paper on "Small Holdings in India and Their Remedies" was published in the first volume of the famous journal of the Indian Economic Society. In 1923 his thesis, "The Problem of the Rupee" was accepted for degree of D. Sc. (Economics) by the London School of Economics. On 15th December, 1925, as an economist he was called by the Hilton Young Commission on Indian Currency and Finance to give evidence.

He tackled the problems of *Mahar watan,* (slavery of untouchables) small holdings, the *khoti* (landlordism) system in Bombay province, landless labourers, land reforms, population control, modes of farming and industrialization of agriculture. To end the serfdom of agricultural tenants by conferring them the occupancy rights, as a legislator in Bombay Legislative Assembly, he introduced a bill for the abolition of *khoti* (*zamandari*), on 17th September, 1937 and became the first legislator in the country to introduce such radical legislation. Apart from the bill, he also build-up the mass struggle, to end the *khoti* system.

Over-Population or population explosion affects development, therefore, on 10th November, 1938 in Bombay Legislative Assembly Dr. Ambedkar introduced the Birth Control Bill. Justifying the Bill he argued, "Want of sufficient capital and rich customers would prevent any material development of our industries. Similarly, insufficiency of infertile lands, rain-fall and manures stand in the way of substantial increase in our agricultural production…. Through the excessive growth of population, our country suffers from deficiency of forests and pasture lands". In a country like India, where children have been considered as the gifts of God and also wealth, introducing the bill, suggesting the measures for birth control was revolutionary effort by Dr. Ambedkar.

From 1942 to 1946, Dr. Ambedkar was in the Viceroy's Council as an in-charge for the departments of labour, water irrigation and electricity. During these 4 years period by his remarkable contribution he laid down the foundations of India's water policy, water transport system, development of energy resources, the management of inter-state river projects, Damodar valley corporation project, other river projects, in 1945 India's first water commission, and many more things. For Ambedkar's involvement in Damodar valley project Lord Casey, the then Governor of Bengal acknowledged Ambedkar's knowledge, competence and wisdom. He remarked, "If I were untouchable, I would have accepted him as my leader and none else"[7].

In States and Minorities, Dr. Ambedkar, in his submission to the Constituent Assembly proposed the scheme of State Socialism, that is, state owned key industries, agriculture as a state industry and collective farming, leaving the scope for private enterprise.[8] Dr. Ambedkar explained, "State socialism is essential for rapid industrialization of India. Private enterprise cannot do it and if it did, it would produce those inequalities of wealth which private capitalism has produced in Europe and which should be a warning to all Indians." In fact, even the National planning committee in 1940, also proposed for state socialism, with state ownership of key industries, collective cultivation of wastelands, cooperative farming, etc. Looking at the present economic inequality in India, wherein almost few individuals who tops the Forbe's list of richest persons in the world as a result of India's rapidly expanding economy without a broad-based industrial revolution, Dr. Ambedkar's advice could be hardly ignored!

Economist Dr. B. R. Ambedkar presented the entire scheme of economic planning not only to the Constituent Assembly but also to Pandit Nehru. However Nehru's response to the scheme was most unfortunate. In his reply to Ambedkar demands, Nehru who was more influenced by the ideas of Fabian socialism explained his inability to confirm any of them.[9] The worst part of the whole episode was that although Dr. Ambedkar was the Chairman of the Drafting Committee of the Constitution, his scheme was not allowed to be discussed both in the advisory committee as well as at the fundamental rights sub-committee. To be fair, Nehru had tried land reforms to end feudal spectrum, the notorious landlordism but he refused to support Dr. Ambedkar's move for the appointment of a separate committee on economic planning. Prime Minister Nehru expressed his fear to Dr. Ambedkar in a communication that, "if we tackle, at this stage, very fundamental economic issues in the process of constitution-making, we might add to the strength of the disruptive tendencies and achieve nothing at all."[10] Had the Constituent Assembly accepted Dr. Ambedkar's view on economic democracy, the face of not only the Constitution but today's economic policy would have been much different from what it is. But the nation neglected Ambedkar. Ultimately Congress-Nehru's leadership proved the saying that, 'power and wisdom hardly goes together'.

In 1945, much before the writing of State and Minorities, Dr. Ambedkar stressed on the State interventionist role in planning economic life of people. He said, "Planned economic development should not only develop programmes, but translate them in terms which the common man could understand, namely, peace, housing and enough clothing, education good health and, above all, the right to work with dignity. The State could not be contended with securing merely fair conditions of work for labour but fair conditions of life. A great responsibility lays on the State to provide the poor with facilities for the growth of individuals according to their needs. To do that end, the government could not be a government of 'laissez faire'; it would have to be a government essentially on a system of control"[11].

Soon after independence, India erred in adopting the model of capital intensive industrial growth neglecting the development of India's rural economy, especially agriculture, unsuited to the social, economic and cultural milieu of country, without taking into account its huge human capital and strength in agriculture sector.[12] But Ambedkar's developmental theory was based on the development of both, industry as well as agriculture.

Therefore, Dr. Ambedkar rightly focused on prominent role of the State with mixture of public and private partnership in nation building. In Small Holding in India, Dr. Ambedkar logically proved that how India's bad social economy is responsible for the ills of Indian agriculture. Dr. Ambedkar concluded his paper, Small Holdings in India, with the observation of Sir Henry Cotton on Indian agriculture. He said there is danger of too much agriculture in India. What Ambedkar talked about the problems of small holdings, way back in 1990 renowned agricultural scientist Dr. M. S. Swaminathan stated, that over 80 million out of the 90 million population of India depend on agriculture.

Due to governmental neglect of agriculture sector, India since last two and half decades is facing the worst of its kind agrarian crisis forcing lakhs of poor farmers to end their lives by committing suicides. India's agricultural problems are multiplied along with low productivity, small holding, agriculture unemployment, more dependence on agriculture, modernization of agriculture, marketism of agriculture produce and above all the anti-farmer governmental policy of minimum support price to farm products. To make further mockery of land reforms, the governmental policy of land acquisition and developmental model has resulted into deprivation of lands to farmers and mass displacement.

Overall the backbone of Ambedkar's developmental model is planned economy with positive interventionist state role cantered with poor people in addition to special treatment for oppressed sections. He was of the opinion that merely industrial development or creation of wealth is not enough but there should be an equitable distribution of the fruits of such development and wealth to the last man of nation.

Going by his perspective, in the age of Liberalization, Privatization and Globalization, (LPG) where are we? Probably because "We the people of India collapsed on political priorities and the great Indian middle class succumbed to the globophonic opium of consumerism. Short term loans recklessly borrowed, were repaid by an irresponsibly   myopic methodology of huge world bank borrowing….Indian political leaders and economic captions jettisoned the concern for Indian humanity's vast but deprived millions, betrayed the commitments regarding the public sector and self reliance, reversed the state obligation to wipeout illiteracy and poverty, to distribute the land for landless to forbid concentration of wealth and means of productions to the common detriment".[13]

2. Dr. Ambedkar on Constitution and Democracy.

The great political thinker Plato in his famous work 'Republic' has referred to democracy as "a charming form of government, full of variety and disorder." But he was prompt enough to point out that, "the laws of democracy remain a dead letters; its freedom is anarchy; its equality the equality of unequals, where even horses and asses claim all the rights and dignities of free citizens."

Being an ethnologist, Dr. Babasaheb Ambedkar was well aware of the casteist cultural background in which the new Constitution and democracy will have to operate. Having realized this he said, "While we have established political democracy, it is also the desire that we should lay down as our ideal economic democracy. We do not want merely to lay down a mechanism to enable people to come and capture power. The Constitution also wished to lay down an ideal before those who would be forming the Government. The ideal is economic democracy...."[14]

In sequel to this, on the day of adoption of the Constitution itself, after urging the countrymen to make political democracy a social democracy as well, with great courage and conviction Ambedkar reminded the people of the country that," We must begin by acknowledging the fact that there is complete absence of two things in the Indian society. One of these is equality. On the social plane, we have in India a society based on the principle of graded inequality which means elevation for some and degradation for others. On the economic plane, we have a society in which there are some who have immense wealth as against many who live in abject poverty. On the 26th of January 1950, we are going to enter into a life of contradictions. In politics we will have equality and in social and economic life we will have inequality. In politics we will be recognizing the principle of one man one vote and one vote one value. In our social and economic life, we shall, by reason of our social and economic structure, continue to deny the principle of one man one value. How long shall we continue to live this life of contradictions? How long shall we continue to deny equality in our social and economic life? If we continue to deny it for long, we will do so only by putting our democracy in peril. We must remove this contradiction at the earliest possible moment or else those who suffer from inequality will blow up the structure of political democracy which this Assembly has so laboriously built up."[15] Whether Indian policy makers, power structure, *Mandir-Masjid-Shilanyas* fundamentalist culture of some political parties and citizens as a whole have paid little attention to these warnings of Dr. Ambedkar? Certainly each one of us will have to ponder over it.

Looking at the anti-democratic, parochial tendencies of political players in the country, Dr. Ambedkar boldly warned them not to place their caste and creed above the nation's interest. He appealed his countrymen to adopt constitutional methods to resolve their issues and abandon the methods like *satyagraha,* non co-operation and other methods. He called such methods as nothing but the Grammer of anarchy. But today everywhere coercive methods and indiscriminate flouting of authority has become a normal practice, although it is against the constitutional spirit, rule of law and democracy.

He warned the countrymen not to practice *Bhakti* in politics, by saying that although may be good in religion. He always considered the Indian communal majority as a potential threat to political majority. In 1955, he said, "majorities are of two sorts: communal majority and political majority. 'A political majority is changeable in its class composition. A political majority grows. A communal majority is born. The admission to a political majority is open. The door to a communal majority is closed. The politics of a political majority are free to all to make and unmake. The politics of a communal majority are made by its own members born in it."

In his one of the best speeches on democracy[16], Dr. Ambedkar held the view that democracy is not a static form of government and with the change of time it may also change in the same country. After taking the review of the definitions of Walter Beghehot[17] and Abrham Lincoln[18], he offered his own definition as it "is a form and method of Government whereby revolutionary changes in the economic and social life of the people are brought about without bloodshed".

Looking at the current scenario, one feels as to how apt was he in his assessment? When India is confronted with the problems of terrorism, naxalism, communalism, politics without morality and other violent means to further issues it has weakened the constitutional democratic framework of India. Looking at the present political culture in the country- solely guided by the mainstream political parties, reminds us of the famous words of former US President, Bill Clinton in his 1992 presidency election campaign when he referred 'The economy stupid', in India it a case of 'The politics, stupid'. Therefore, Dr. Ambedkar, in his intellectual discourse, considered an absence of glaring inequalities in the society and presence of equality in law and administration, strict observance of constitutional morality and the most vital thing is that in the name of democracy there must be no tyranny of the majority over the minority.

Dr. Ambedkar was internationally an acclaimed jurist. Being the chief architect of the Constitution, he was described by some as a modern law-giver. On his death, the international edition of "The New York Times", described him as follows: "What is perhaps not so well known is that he put a profound impress upon India's major legal structures. As the Minister of Law in Mr. Nehru's Cabinet, he was one of the real authors of the Indian Constitution. More than that, he was the principal draftsman of the statutory "Hindu Code" whose purpose was to change, under Law, some of the basic framework of the Indian Society and to move it into a more liberal and humanistic pattern."[19] Therefore, even his strong critics, like Syamanandan Sahay- a member of the Constituent Assembly- aptly said, "The achievement of independence would go to the credit of Mahatmaji and its codification to one of Mahatmaji's worst critics, viz. the great architect of our Constitution, Dr. Ambedkar".[20]

Justice Billings Learned Hand -an American judge and judicial philosopher in his short speech, on 'The Spirit of

Liberty,' May 21, 1944, at New York on "American Day", has rightly said, "Liberty lives in the hearts of men and women, if it lives there, there is no need of law, court and the Constitution. But if it dies there, no law, no court, no Constitution can protect it". Dr. Ambedkar was well aware of this reality. Therefore he favoured the creation of a social environment wherein liberty as well as fraternity will blossom and facilitate all round development of the citizens. He was prompt in reminding the rulers that no nation founded upon injustice can permanently stand.[21]

Dr. Ambedkar wanted India to embrace socio-economic democracy, to transform its traditional unequal social order into a humanitarian one, and to make every Indian a true partner in the governing process and an equal beneficiary in the development process by using constitutional means. He strived for structural changes, peaceful socio-economic change and empowerment of all.

Dr. Ambedkar expected the governing class to consider the Constitution as a document of faith and conviction and not as a matter of mere convenience. He expected the people of India to rise up to the level of constitutional morality and culture. Probably, he was not sure and hence observed, "I feel the Constitution is workable, flexible and good enough to hold the country together both in peace time and in war time. Indeed, if I may say so, if things go wrong under the new Constitution, the reason will not be that we had a bad Constitution. What we will have to say is that man was vile".[22]   The caste and communal loyalties, barring few occasions, have reduced the Indian democracy and the constitution to a farce, compelling someone to jokingly remark that, 'In India you do not cast your vote, you vote your caste'[23].

In the 21st century, when India is speedily marching towards global competitive liberal market economy with rising number of millionaires and successful upper middle class but paradoxically excluding the poor, marginalized downtrodden- far away from the very human existence as well as basic human rights, the constitutional cry of reordering India-socially, economically and politically remains as the core of India's overall real development and so also Dr. B. R. Ambedkar's constitutional vision. The constitutional developments in India in the last 70 years, the mountening number of constitutional amendments-some desired, some unwanted, constitutional-governmental-judicial crises- creations of unconstitutional behaviour of constitutional functionaries and even on some occasions the collective silence from "We the People" of India have proved Ambedkar's prophecy right.

3. Dr. Ambedkar on Indian Villages:

The advocates of the Indian village system, including Mr. M. K. Gandhi considered villages as independent republics. Even today's majority of urban elites are very fond of villages and continue to subscribe to the Gandhian love to the villages, although villages have become outing spots for most of them. Roughly India's 1.2 billion people live in near about 680,000 villages, without even elementary schools, healthcare centers and in the worst culture of chronic poverty, caste, untouchability and exploitation.

In India and abroad, Gandhism "has become popular for journalists and academicians to write off Gandhi's philosophy as officially dead. Certainly, as a political ideology, Gandhism in current Indian politics is an orphan; none of India's many political parties officially endorse the Gandhian philosophy of the village. But as a social attitude his view of the village lives on notably in much of India's civil service; it can be heard coming from the mouths of many of India's senior diplomats and judges and it is still mainstream among India's non-governmental organizations...."[24] Although Gandhism has been completely written off, though the so-called Gandhians keep on chanting the Gandhi mantra which reminds the saying of great scientist Albert Einstein that 'insanity was doing the same thing over and over again and expecting different results'.

During the constitution making process, several members were keen to make the Indian village as the basic unit of Indian polity. Dr. Rajendra Prasad too, in his letter of 10th May, 1948 to Shri. B. N. Rau, expressed his desire of making the Constitution to begin with the village and go up to the Centre. Naturally, some members in the Constituent Assembly, especially Gandhians, demanded the village system as the basic unit of constitutional structure. But Dr. Ambedkar being westernized in outlook and a radical democrat, perceived the ancient village *Panchayat* system as an antithesis to the democratic culture. In contrast to the strong views of some of the Congressmen that villages have been ancient independent republics, Dr. Ambedkar stood like the China wall against their views.

While moving the Draft Constitution, on 4th November, 1948, he condemned in strong words the love of Indians for the village system. He said, "The love of the intellectual Indian for the village community is of of course infinite-if not pathetic. It is largely due to the fulsome praise bestowed upon it by Metcalfe who described them as little republics

32

having nearly everything that they want within themselves, and almost independent of any foreign relations. The existence of these village communities, each one forming a separate little State in itself, has according to Metcalfe contributed more than any other cause to the preservation of the people of India through all the revolutions and changes which they have suffered and is in a high degree conducive to their happiness and to the enjoyment of a great portion of their freedom and independence. No doubt the village communities have lasted where nothing else lasts. But those who take pride in the villages communities do not care to consider what little part they have played in the affairs and destiny of the country; and why? Their part in the destiny of the country has been well described by Metcalfe himself who says: "Dynasty after dynasty tumbles down. Revolution succeeds to revolution. Hindoo, Pathan, Mogul, Maratha, Sikh, English, are all masters in turn but the village communities remain the same. In times of trouble they arm and fortify themselves. A hostile army passes through the country. The village communities collect their little cattle within their walls and let the enemy pass unprovoked."

Before Dr. Ambedkar's strong criticism about villages in the Constituent Assembly, in his one of the earliest writings between 1913-1915, "Ancient Indian Commerce", he had referred the village system in India. It was followed by another work, "Administration and Finance of the East India Company" his dissertation to Columbia University for his M.A. degree in Economic, in 1915, describing about villages. In fact that description of Dr. Ambedkar is more or less like Marx's description of villages in the first volume of 'Das Capital'.[25] Again while speaking in Bombay Legislative Assembly on Village Panchayat Bill in 1932, he said, " If India has not succeded in producing nationalism, if India has not succeeded in building up a national spirit, the chief reason for that in my opinion is that the existence of the village system. It made all people saturated with local particularim, with local patriotism".[26] Thus, Dr. Ambedkar concluded that the excessive village patriotism and village spirit proved very fatal to the growth of strong Indian nationality.

In the Constituent Assembly, while moving the Draft Constitution, on 4th November, 1948, Dr. Ambedkar again echoed his thoughts about villages and said, "such is the part the villages have played in the history of their country. Knowing this, what pride can one feel in them? That they have survived through all vicissitudes may be a fact. But mere survival has no value. The question is on what plane they have survived. Surely on a low, on a selfish level. I hold that these village republics have been the ruination of India. I am therefore surprised that those who condemn provincialism and communalism could come forward as champions of the village. What is the village but a sink of localism, a den of ignorance, narrow mindedness and communalism? I am glad that the Draft Constitution has discarded the village and adopted the individual as its unit".[27]

4. Dr. Ambedkar on Governance:

Dr. Ambedkar's idea of government was not confined merely to 'rule' but constitutional mechanism for the socio-economic democracy. Way back in 1930, he stated, "We must have a Government in which the men in power will give their undivided allegiance to the best interest of the country,. We must have a government in which men in power, knowing where obedience will end and resistance will begin, will not be afraid to amend, the social and economic code of life which dictates of justice and expediency so urgently call for"[28]

Although this was said by Dr. Babasaheb to the British government in 1930, it also applies to the present governments in India. Even after 70 years of constitutional governance in India, by and large, general mass is far away from the governmental business, living a customary life of nomad in far remote territorial areas of India. Going by the dismissal performance of the rulers, those who are away from the corridors of power structure expect least from governance. Sometimes, men in governance have developed the habit of pacifying the people by saying that the British left our country as an empty shell, with the resources undeveloped, with the people of this country untrained for economic production.

But while speaking on the address of the President of India in Rajya Sabha on 21 May, 1952, Dr. Ambedkar warned the government arguing that, "No hungry man is going to be sympathetic to a critic who is going to tell him –My dear fellow, although I am in power, although I am in authority, although I possess all legal power to set matters right, you must not expect me to do a miracle because I have inherited a past which is very inglorious"[29]. Further he said that if the government doesn't produce results within certain time people will be frustrated, disgusted with the governments as to not have the government at all. That contention of Dr. Ambedkar answers the query of an s ordinary common Indian, as to what is the use of the government? Dr. Ambedkar, in his speech referred to the shortage of food grains and expected from Prime Minister Nehru a promise of self sufficiency in food in 1952, in 1956, if not in the year 1960. Looking at the prevailing pathetic situation of agriculture, inflation and shortage of food grains in 2009, especially when nearly 41% Indians live below the poverty line, there is an absolute need to understand Dr. Ambedkar's perspective.

5. Dr. Ambedkar on India's Foreign Policy.

Recently in a matter of major concern on the front of national foreign affairs, China in the month of November, 2009, on three occasions took an open stand against India. First it objected to Prime Minister Manmohan Singh's visit to Arunachal Pradesh stating that the "Boarder State is our land of rising sun". In another case, China strongly objected even Dalai Lama's visit to Arunachal Pradesh and expressed "strong concern" over his visit, saying it "further reveals the Dalai clique's anti-China and separatist essence". In what is seen as yet another example of China showing its assertiveness, the then Jammu and Kashmir Government on the earlier day had stopped work on a strategic road project after the Chinese indicated their reservations over the same. The state government confirmed that the work was stopped on a road project under the National Rural Employment Guarantee Scheme (NREGS), in south-east Leh in Ladakh, after the Chinese army objected.

Historically, China has been Pakistan's strategic and military ally for the past 50 years. It was China who gave Pakistan the designs for a nuclear bomb in 1984 and then helped them to build it. China also assisted Pakistan by providing missile technology via North Korea, Chinese-made fighter jets and specialized small arms. China has two purposes behind its assistance to Pakistan. First, it takes Pakistan as a secure friend and ally in the Indian Ocean and second, they share a common interest to contain India.

Dr. Ambedkar was very vocal in attacking Nehru's foreign policy. When people were wanting to remain in Nehru's cabinet, Ambedkar in the nation's interest and for just reasons resigned from his cabinet. According to him one of the reasons was that of Nehru's faulty foreign policy. He said, on 15th August, 1947, at the time of independence we had no enemy country, but in a span of only four years our friend countries have deserted us, we have not even have a one friendly country to second our resolutions in the UNO.[30] Quoting famous sayings of Bismark[31] and Barnard Shaw[32], he said, our foreign policy is in complete opposition to these words of wisdom uttered by two of the worlds greatest men. He also challenged Nehru's policy statement that we have no enemy nation on which he questioned him then that out of 350 crores revenue why are we spending about Rs. 180 crores, colossal expenditure on the Army.

Again on 26th August, 1954, Dr. Ambedkar, in Council of States, in very strong words and by citing different country's examples criticized Pandit Nehru's governmental foreign policy. He warned the government that, 'by allowing China to take over Tibet, already China has reached near the boarder of India and hence we should not tolerate China. He also warned Nehru by saying that don't take *Panchsheel* seriously in international politics, especially when you are dealing with a communist country. He said, "The *Panchasheel* is the essential part of the Buddhist religion, and if Mr. Mao had any faith in the Panchasheel, he certainly would treat the Buddhists in his own country in a very different manner. There is no room for *Panchasheel* in politics and secondly, not in the politics of a communist country".[33] But Nehru and the Congress Party at the Centre continued the same policy though *Hindi- Chini Bhai Bhai* till China attacked India in 1962. The same international ghost is now gunning against India. Just think, had Nehru considered Ambedkar's view on China, perhaps 1962 and subsequent problematic international issues, definitely would not have come up to the present level.

6. Dr. Ambedkar and Labour Movement in India.

Where was Ambedkar in 1942?[34] Normally even an ordinary idiotic man may not dare to pose such a question about Ambedkar, that too in 1997, when government of Maharashtra had already published bulky volume of 1080 pages, numbered 10 in the series of publications on Dr. Ambedkar. But in India there is no dearth of such species. Yes, along with other Indians Ambedkar became the member of Viceroy's cabinet on 20th July, 1942, when Congress passed the famous resolution in Bombay "quit India" on 9 August, 1942. In the cabinet, from 1942 to 1946, he was the minister for Labour, Water and Electricity laying down the foundations of modern temples[35] of India and labour jurisprudence.

In 1938, much before, Dr. Ambedkar's labour minister-ship in Viceroy's executive council, in 1935 Dr. Ambedkar had formed Independent Labour Party, his first political party, to pursue the demands of untouchables, peasants and workers. In September, 1938, in the Bombay Assembly, the then Congress government introduced the most notorious bill, i.e. Industrial Disputes Bill-prohibiting the workers to go on strike under certain circumstances. Dr. Ambedkar and his party opposed the bill. Dr. Ambedkar described the Bill as, "bad, bloody and bloodthirsty in as must as it made a strike under certain circumstances illegal and affected the right of the labourer to strike". In justification of workers right to go on strike he said, making a man serve against his will was nothing less than making him a slave….If the Congressmen accepted that the right to freedom was a divine right then, the right to strike was also a divine right of workers".

During Ambedkar's term in Viceroy's council, under his dynamic leadership, India commenced the foundational work of rebuilding India, through the water policy, central water commission, *Damodar* irrigation valley project-the first biggest Hydro-electrical multipurpose power project, *Hirakud* and Son rivers project. On 3rd January, 1944 at Calcutta, he explained that the object of *Damodar* project is not only to control water flood but also to generate power, to create a big reservoir for irrigation and industrialization, water navigation. Because of the most dynamic leadership of Dr. Ambedkar, in less than four years, this giant project was completed and handed over to the nation.

Professor H. C. Hurt, author of the *'Rivers of India'* appreciating the role of Dr. Ambedkar said, "The thirty months of planning of the *Damodar* properly fell into the hands of politicians. There were men equal to the task. But the man who in the political sense decided that the *Damodar* would be controlled, was the Minister of Labour in the pre-Independence Cabinet, Dr. B. R. Ambedkar".[36] Even before leaving the ministry in June, 1946 he had prepared detailed programme for the rehabilitation of the project affected people, which include adequate land, sufficient housing and other facilities. That became the guiding policy for all the provincial governments to implement their rehabilitation policy.

In 1946, when C. H. Bhabha received the charge of ministry from Ambedkar, he remarked, "in shortest time we have moved from the medieval traditional concepts to modern water development concept and planned for development this project. In this the first conference (under president-ship of Dr. Ambedkar, at Calcutta, on January 3, 1944.) was very significant. Because that conference guided, *Mahanadi, Kosi* and *Son* river projects. For that we thank those who done everything for such multipurpose regional developmental projects"[37].

In December, 1945 in the conference called for Multipurpose Plan for Development of Orissa's Rivers at Cuttack, Dr Ambedkar, after taking the stock of failed efforts by all earlier authorities from 1872 to 1945 he remarked, "With all respect to the members of these committees, I am sorry to say that they did not bring the right approach to bear on the problem. They were influenced by the idea that the water in the excessive quantity was an evil, that when water comes in excessive quantity, what needs to be done is to let it run into the sea in an orderly flow. Both these views are now regarded as grave misconceptions, as positively dangerous from the point of the good of the people....water being the wealth of the people and its distribution being uncertain, the correct approach is not to complain against nature but to conserve water".[38] While concluding the speech in beautiful expression he said, "other engineers may give us speed in travel or comfort in our dwellings; your gift is that of life itself. If you want a text for your labours you will find it in a verse of Isaiah; 'I give waters in the wilderness and rivers in the desert, to give to drink my people".[39]

Along with such historical national duty, Dr. Ambedkar was deeply involved in building a new labour jurisprudence for India. . His tenure as Labour Member in the Viceroy's Council during 1942-46 was a watershed in the history of labour legislation, welfare and labour movement in India. He adopted a multi-pronged approach in the formulation of labour policy with provisions for: providing safeguard and social security measures for workers; giving equal

45

opportunity to workers and employers to participate in the formulation of labour policy; and establishing a machinery for enforcing labour laws and settling disputes He held the view that, unemployment and underemployment were the greatest enemies of labour. As a consequence he tried to formulate a full employment policy for labour and a state supported labour welfare system.

From uniformity of labour legislations to warning the labouring class to discard the mere establishment of Trade Unions as the final aim and object of Labour in India and develop an ambition for capturing the government as a necessary means of safeguarding their interests.[40] On 6th and 7th September, 1943, in the second sessions of the tripartite labour conference, as a president of conference, Dr. Ambedkar strongly demanded basic amenities for labours.

7. Dr. Ambedkar and Empowerment of Powerless.

By and large, so called Indian intellectuals have failed to take into account Ambedkar's perspective on national interest or freedom movement and goal of empowering the powerless, the cause lovable to Ambedkar's heart.

There was never a clash in between the two. Therefore, on 26th April, 1942 he openly said to the Congress Party that, "You are fighting for *swaraj*. I am ready to join you. And I may assure you that I can fight better than you. I make only one condition. Tell me what share I am to have in *swaraj*"[41]. In his pragmatic approach Dr. Ambedkar was more guided by the Greek historian Thucydides who said, "It may lie in your interest to be our masters but how can it be in our interests to be your slaves".

The ideological foundation of his movement can be gathered from the teachings of Buddha, Phuley and Kabir as well as from his writings, speeches and timely social and political actions. Both the *'Castes In India-Their Mechanism, Genesis and Development'*, a paper, Ambedkar read before an anthropology seminar at the Columbia University, USA, on 9th May, 1916, and his undelivered speech titled, *'Annihilation of Caste'* for the 1936 annual conference of the *Jat-Pat Todak Mandal* of Lahore, clearly provide the necessity of a social revolution in the country from the victims of caste culture.

Dr. Ambedkar's unfinished agenda of caste-free society has aptly reiterated by the Apex Court of India, while deciding the case of 30 years back *Dalit* massacre in Uttar Pradesh. The Court in its decision, on 5th December, 2009, has observed, "It is absolutely imperative to abolish the caste system as expeditiously as possible for smooth functioning of rule of law and democracy in our country".[42] Even after the 62 years of India's independence, such verdict and observation coming from the highest court of country proves that Dr. Ambedkar's "freedom struggle" was much greater and bigger in size than the so-called nationalists "freedom struggle".

Unlike most of the social reformers, Ambedkar's quest was to empower the powerless sections of Indian society, socially, educationally, economically, politically and culturally too. Therefore, from education to conversion and from reservation policy to political power, Dr. Ambedkar waged a war against the overall monopoly of so-called upper castes in India so as to rebuild it on equalitarian plain. From Hindu Code Bill, People's Education Society to the concept of Republican Party, the entire process, he lead from the front not merely like sermonic messages by some other Indian leaders. From separate electorate scheme he also designed the scheme of separate settlement for the Scheduled Castes to end their age-old oppression. He argued, that there were large areas of cultivable waste land lying untenanted in the country which could be set apart for the settlements of Scheduled Castes and the village being a social and not economic unit of society, there was no need to fear economic strangulation of these separate villages.[43] unfortunately it could not materialize in his life time.

After the three Round Table Conference held in London between British Government and the Indian leaders, Dr. Ambedkar's demand of separate electorate was accepted by the British government and had made a declaration to that effect on August 17, 1932 which is popularly known as, "communal award." Congress leader M. K. Gandhi was opposed to the idea. On failure of Gandhi's attempt to defeat Dr. B. R. Ambedkar and the just claims of the depressed classes in the Round Table deliberations led him to commence his infamous 'fast unto death' on September 20, 1932 in the Yervada prison in Pune. The coercive fast of the leader of the so-called non-violence movement forced the depressed classes and Dr. Ambedkar to accept joint electorate and give up their right of separate electorate which came to be known as the Poona Pact. Gandhi never went on a fast unto death against British for swaraj. Among all his fasts, his only fast unto death was against Dr. Ambedkar and the untouchables. Because Gandhi knew that Ambedkar was a political liberal and political liberals cannot comfortably face opponents who undertake to die for a cause; nor could they themselves offer to destroy themselves in like fashion. Gandhi gambled on Babasaheb's goodness.[44]

At his point, it is absolutely essential to know that, to attain the objectives, Dr. Ambedkar adopted all kinds of ideas and strategies, sometimes in the most violent manner, accusing the M.K. Gandhi and other frontline leadership of the Congress party in the most bitter words. Whenever he thought a necessity to reconcile with other forces in the country he compromised with them but never pursued the anti India path or compromised with anti national elements or directed his millions of followers throughout the country towards the theory of a separate nation, like Mohammad Ali Jinnah and others. Unfortunately some people in India are still unable to understand this nationalist Ambedkar-the great patriot.

8. Dr. Ambedkar and Cultural Revolution of Buddhism.

Dr. Ambedkar had an ardent desire to take up his socio-cultural revolt up to a logical end. Throughout his life when he waged a war against *Brahminism* how he leave his people at the mercy to the same way of life they led. Therefore it was but natural that his movement should culminate into a cultural revolution, that is, an alternative culture to the Hindu way of life. In that direction, Dr. Ambedkar pursued the agenda of a cultural revolution in a very systematic manner since 1924.

According to Kal Marx a German Philosopher "religion is the opium of the masses." In contrast to Marxist approach, religion, Dr. Ambedkar, considered as one of the requirement of human life. Like Irish statesman and philosopher Edmund Burke's view he held that every society needs a religion. In 'Philosophy of Hinduism', Ambedkar denounced the idea that all religions are equally good and that there is no necessity of discrimination between them as the most harmful false notion. Therefore, as an alternate way of life to millions of suffering people in India, Dr. Ambedkar's scientific, and pragmatic way of thinking led to redefining Buddhism and embracing Buddhism with lakhs of followers at Nagpur on 14th

October, 1956. Buddha's opposition to casteism, priest-craft, Buddhism's features, such as, atheism, secular character, law of reasoning against superstitions, *panchasheel, maitri, karuna* morality attracted rationalist Ambedkar. Liberty, equality, fraternity and justice to all, these four postulates of Buddhism had a profound influence on him. Yet Ambedkar's modern outlook rejected the traditional Buddhism and gave a way to Ambedkar's Buddha and his Dhamma. Ipso-facto, Buddha and His Dhamma is an evidence of Dr. Ambedkar's journey towards the redefined Buddhism which has provided the new foundations to Buddhism in India.

In 1881, Sir William Hunter, Member of Indian Civil Service and as a member of the governor-general's council, presided over the Commission on Indian Education; in 1886 he was elected vice-chancellor of the University of Calcutta had made a prophecy about the revival of Buddhism in India. Gurudeo Ravindranath Tagore who was deeply influenced by the life and philosophy of Budha, in one of his poems "Buddhadeo" expected the revival of Buddhism in India. Dr. Ambedkar's embracing Buddhism fulfilled the dreams of two great scholars. But in compare to all other conversion movements, Ambedkar's acceptance to Buddhism was viewed by many from different angles but for Ambedkar it was a mass action for social respect-liberation from the traditional bonds of slavery of Brahmanical Hinduism. Mr. V. D. Savarkar, the face of Hindu fundamentalist Nationalism openly opposed Ambedkar's move of reviving Buddhism in India, whereas, leaders like Nehru, Dr. Prasad, and even Dr. Radhakrishnan did not even wish Dr. Ambedkar for such a peaceful cultural revolution.

When Dr. Ambedkar's movement of Buddhism was opposed by conservative Hindus on several grounds, he said, throughout the world people revolt against exploitation. This is natural in the course of history. In Mumbai, from 30th May to 2 June, 1936, in the four days conference, Ambedkar in his famous speech *"Mukti Kon Pathe"* (which way Liberation) explained the whole world that without any materialist gain what was the object of joining the fold of Buddhism, but unfortunately many are yet to grasp it. Dr. Ambedkar viewed Buddhism as the means of reconstruction of Indian society, premised on values of Liberty, Equality, Fraternity and Justice to all.

Before conversion, Dr. Ambedkar considered Buddhism as a potential alternative to *Brahminism*. In his writing 'Revolution and Counter Revolution in Indian Society' he said, "the history of Indian society is a history of conflict between *Brahminism* and Buddhism." At the same time, he also viewed *Dhamma* as an alternative model to Marxism. In one of his essays titled 'Buddha and Karl Marx',[45] he pointed out similarity of the doctrines and approaches of Buddha and Karl Marx.

According to Dr. B. R. Ambedkar, the purpose of *religion* was to explain the origin of the world, while the purpose of *Dhamma* was to reconstruct the world. Therefore, he looked towards Buddhism as the necessary and the most effective weapon in the caste-ridden Indian society. That does not mean that Ambedkar accepted the Buddhist way of life as it was prevalent. He gave a new interpretation to the *Dhamma* so as to differentiate its character from the three ways of *Dhamma-Theravada, Mahayana and Vajrayana*. In the preface to the 'The Buddha and His Dhamma', he adopted a radical view about Buddha's *Parivraja* by rejecting the traditional version. He was also frank enough to admit the contradiction between the doctrines of karma, rebirth and Buddha's denial of the existence of the soul. In contrast to the traditional role of *Bhikku (Buddhist monk)*, he believed that the *Bhikku* could be the hope of Buddhism only if he would be a social servant and not a perfect man.[46]

By such unique achievements, without the sanction and support of state power, Dr. Ambedkar attained the leading position among the liberation movements. This bloodless cultural revolution, a silent revolution of the resource-less masses, without the backing of any political power, saw as many as over five lakh people discarding all material considerations embraced Buddhism at Nagpur on October 14, 1956, under his dynamic leadership. This was the golden moment in the history of the world's socio-cultural revolutions. At that meeting Dr. Ambedkar also announced of making the entire India as one Buddhist nation. But, unfortunately he could not live long enough to achieve that.

9. Dr. Ambedkar and Indian Historiography.

It is popularly said that, what memory is to man so history is to mankind. It tells us about the culture and collective conscience of a society, the record of revolutions and counter-revolutions. The construction of history, or history writing in India began with ancient period and in the process of it various perspectives, such as, *brahmanical*, colonial, nationalist, Marxist and subaltern historians have played a significant role. One more aspect of the Indian historiography is that among all perspectives there is one common thing and that is the presentation of history so as to suit their manifold interests.

In India, the general historians are by and large responsible for negligence of subaltern history and also for writing history in '*Aryan*' form. Such so-called historians could be charged for the offence of false story writings and selling historical lies. On this historical non-sense, almost 1000 years ago, Alberuni distinguished himself as a historian, chronologist and linguist and also the Father of modern geodesy", and the first anthropologist had said that, "Indian had achieved so much and so well in so many branches of knowledge, but lacked the historical sense. History writing as the conscious art did not develop in India".[47] D. D.

Kosmabi, a noted thinker and historian has observed, "history is the penetration in the chronological order of successive changes in the means of production any 'personal' 'episodic' drum and trumpet history of India should be enjoyed as romantic fiction or some Indian railway time table".[48] Equally, Mr. R. C. Muzumdar stated, "history divorced from truth, does not help a nation- its future should be laid down on the stable foundations of the truth and not the quicksand's of falsehood, however alluring it may appear at present".[49]

In the light of such historiography, Mahatma Phule, Dr. Ambedkar and other social rebels must be credited for their articulation of neglected history of *Shudras* and *ati-Shudras*. Dr. Ambedkar, without being keen student of history could not have authored historical writings, such as, Who Were the Shudras. By applying the historical as well as analytical methods of research he has not only grasped the Indian history but presented the *Shudra's* history. Therefore, in Who Were the Shudras, he says, "I claim that in my research I have been guided by the best tradition of the historian who treats all literature as vulgar-I am using the word its original sense of belonging to the people –to be examined and tested by accepted rules of evidence without recognizing any distinction between the sacred and profane and with the sole object of finding the truth".[50]

Pointing out the distinction between a *Brahmanic* and non-*Brahmanic* scholar, while studying the problems of the social history of Hindus-the former with his attitude of uncritical commendation and the latter with his attitude of unsparing condemnation is most harmful to historical research and therefore the mischief done by the *Brahmin* scholars to historical research is obvious".[51]

The true spirit of an historian, he said, an historian ought to be exact, sincere, and impartial; free from passion, unbiased by interest, fear, resentment or affection; and faithful to the truth, which is the mother of history, the preserver of great actions, the enemy of oblivion, the witness of the past, the director of the future. In short he must have an open mind, though it may not be an empty mind, and readiness to examine all evidence even though it may be spurious"[52].

In his landmark speech, Ranade, Gandhi and Jinnah, while examining the role of a great man and his relation to history, the unsentimental historian Dr. Ambedkar said, "....There are those who assert that however a great man may be, he is a creature of Time-Time called him forth. Time did everything, he did nothing. Those who hold this view, in my judgment, wrongly interpret history. There have been three different views on the causes of historical changes. We have had the Augustinian theory of history, according to which history is only an unfolding of a divine plan in which mankind is to continue through war and suffering until that divine plan is completed at the day of the judgment. There is the view of the Buckle who held that the history was made by Geography and Physics. Karl Marx propounded a third view. According to him the history was the result of economic forces. None of these three would admit that history is the biography of great men indeed they deny man any place in the making of history. Their views do not represent the whole truth. They are quite wrong in holding that impersonal forces are a determining factor cannot be denied".[53]

This whole analysis of history and historians, their perspectives, shows that how deeply Dr. Ambedkar was involved in the art of history writing, besides making a new history for India.

10. Dr. Ambedkar's Militant Power Discourse.

Dr. Ambedkar, throughout his life strongly articulated the radical but without bloodshed power discourse in the hearts and minds of millions of his followers. In the concluding part of his last speech in the Constituent Assembly, on 25th November, 1949, Dr. Ambedkar stressed on the necessity of sharing a power with down-trodden classes. Dr. Babasaheb held the confirmed view that the destiny of the poor will not change as long as they are not made partners in power. Worried by the monopoly of few castes over power structure he warned the countrymen, "political power in this country has too long been the monopoly of a few and the many are not only beasts of burden but also beasts of pray. The monopoly has not only deprived them of their chances of betterment, it has sapped them of what may be called the significance of life. These down-trodden classes are tired of being governed. They are impatient to govern themselves. This urge for self-realization in the down-trodden classes must not be allowed to be devolved into a class struggle or class war. It would lead to the division of the House.... Therefore the sooner room is made for the realization of their aspiration, the better for the maintenance of its independence, and better for the continuance of its democratic structure".[54]

Dr. Ambedkar in his first political move before the South Borough Committee referred to at the time as the **Franchise Committee**, in 1919, at the age of 28 years, represented the cause of the entire untouchables of the Bombay province disowning the method of making group representations as it was done by the earlier social reformers. In his evidence he strongly argued that, 'Hindus have isolated the untouchables from any kind of social participation, they have been dehumanized by socio-religious disabilities, denied the universally accepted rights of citizens and are reduced to the status of slaves.' In his submission, he also criticized the scheme of the Congress Party which supported the communal representation to the Muslims but denied the same to the untouchables. He strongly objected against the proposal of the Depressed Class Mission led by Mr. V. R. Shinde suggesting for nomination instead of election of untouchable's representative to the imperial council. He also urged the government not to reproduce and perpetuate the social disabilities and hardships of untouchables through political institutions.

From right to vote to capture the political power, Ambedkar fought with his opponents by devising various strategies, without compromising on several issues. Dr Ambedkar's life struggle aimed to destroy the oppressive social order and to bring about an equitable, non –capitalist economic restructuring through mass awakening, by reform as well radical but democratic movements and constitutional transformation.

During Ambedkar's time, since the politics of the Congress, the mouthpiece of the dominant castes was detrimental to the very existence and interests of the backward classes, Dr. Ambedkar in 1949-50 came out with the strategical theory of broad based political coalition of the SCs, STs, OBCs and Religious Minorities. As a part of it, at the Scheduled Castes Federation's Conference (Ambedkar's own political party) in Lucknow, on April 25, 1948 (when he was the law minister in the Nehru cabinet), he said, "The SCs and the BCs form majority of the population of the country. If so, there is no reason why they should not rule this country? All that is necessary is to organize action to capture political power, which is your own, through adult suffrage. People do not seem to buck up courage because they are overwhelmed by the belief that the Congress government is there forever. I say this is a wrong impression. In a popular democracy, no government is permanent; not even the government established by the two of the tallest Congressmen, Pandit Nehru and Sardar Patel. If you organize you can even capture that government."

From historical developments and several other records of struggle by Ambedkar, it is very clear that in his last phase of life, he concentrated more on the political and cultural agenda. He believed firmly that the destiny of disadvantaged poor will not change as long as they are not made partners in power. Thereafter, he continued to speak on the importance of capturing "political power as a master key for social progress".

In his last days of life, he made serious efforts to bring not only the SCs, STs and OBCs under one banner but also the minorities, the victims of *Brahminical* oppression and exploitation. His prime argument was that the victims of the *Brahminical* social order needed strong power to destroy the power on other side because it was power that ultimately made one interest dominant over the other. He was also of the firm belief that in the creation of a new social order, political power was absolutely essential because only rulers could create a new-casteless society. To achieve this he planned to have a broad based political coalition with some socialist leaders, such as, Dr. Ram Manohar Lohia but due to his sudden death on 6th December, 1956, the entire journey, and one golden era in the history of liberation movements came to a halt.

DYNAMICS OF AMBEDKARISM:

Dr. Ambedkar, though out his struggle was dynamic in approach and so never stuck to any single strategy but adopted various techniques to complete his agenda. Therefore, Dr. Ambedkar's liberation movement was dynamic in nature. To achieve its' objects it got adapted to the changing equations-social, economic and political. As a matter of strategy to defeat an enemy in socio-political war as well as to meet out the needs of movement he went on changing even the names of his publications, social organizations and even a political party. Therefore, for the theoreticians, to capture Dr. Ambedkar's multidimensional human rights struggle and appreciate his ideology correctly is a bit difficult task.

Further, Dr. Ambedkar, himself, was not bent upon to formulate a particular theory of human liberation by sitting in the library, but was deeply involved into grass rooted movement, from the process of grass root mobilization of confidence--resource less slaves of the unjust system to make them the rulers of land. Dr. Ambedkar, like Marx, did not spent the major part of his active life in research and writing, but with political activism, the demands of leadership absorbed the major part of his life.

On one hand he was fighting against the social oppressive forces of *Brahmanism-Hindus* as well as political force of Congress-Gandhi reformist Hindus, on the other hand he was preparing the downtrodden mass for the struggle and pursued the British to concede to his demands. His main concern was not to philsophise or interprets the surrounding world, but to change it.

Dr. Ambedkar's revolt, Ambedkarism, is the reconstructive ideology with an agenda of annihilation of caste, anti-caste struggle in sequel to the socio-cultural revolts of Charvaka, Buddha, Mahatma Phuley, Kabir and all those who revolted against the inhuman varna-caste culture. However, in some of the matters, Dr. Ambedkar has dealt it independently. Dr. Ambedkar's canvass of activity was so vast and of multi-dimensional nature that it becomes difficult for any scholar to grasp him in its entirety. He has struggled, written and spoken so much on divergent subjects and in changing contexts that naturally tempts any scholar to level a charge of inconsistency on him. But it is also worthwhile to see that such a charge is coming from which quarter-Leftists, Rightist, Centrists or from fundamentalist Hindu.

CONCLUSION-

From the above lined glimpses of Dr. Ambedkar's life, struggle and philosophy one can gather that by his yeoman services he has immensely contributed to modern India. Going by the above most concise presentation nobody can dare to think that his life-struggle was merely confined to ex-untouchable's liberation or empowerment. By rebuilding the neglected India, he has strengthened the modern India.

Dr. Ambedkar, in his entire analysis of either *Brahmanical* scriptures or Gandhi and Congress, there was never an element of remote enmity but the venture was guided by national interest. Knowing the degree of opposition, he was frank enough to say that, "I do not care for the credit which every progressive society must give to its rebels. I shall be satisfied if I make the Hindus realize that they are the sick men of India and that their sickness is causing danger to the health and happiness of other Indians".[55] While opposing M. K. Gandhi or Barrister Jinnah, he was quite vocal in saying that, "I insist that if I hate Mr. Gandhi and Mr. Jinnah-I dislike them, I do not hate them -it is because I love India more. That is the true faith of a nationalist. I have hopes that my countrymen, will someday learn that the country is greater than the men, that the worship of Mr. Gandhi or Mr.

Jinnah and service to India are two very different things and may even be contradictory of each other".[56]

"Annihilation of Caste", undelivered speech of Dr. Ambedkar in 1936, represent one of the glorious monuments in philosophical analysis of Indian social system. In that speech on one hand he warned socialists that, "you turn in any direction, caste is the monster that crosses your each and every path", and on other hand he countered Mr. Surendranath Bannerji former Congress President by saying that, "Are you fit for political power even though you do not allow a large class of your own countrymen like the untouchables to use public school, public wells, public streets". Like a roaring lion he thundered, every Congressman who repeats the dogma of Mill (John Stuart Mill) that one country is not fit to rule another country must admit that one class is not fit to rule another class".[57]

In his economic analysis of British Empire in India, he with a great courage and conviction held the British policy responsible for the strengthening the caste mechanism, and for the destruction of trade, commerce and artisans life in India. However due to the anti untouchable policy of Gandhi and Congress made him to depend upon the British for necessary help in his mission. Despite the fact, nationalist

Ambedkar worked in the company of Congressmen to produce the Constitution of India-one of the finest constitutions in the world.

Dr. Ambedkar's act of revival of 2500 years old Buddhism, participation in a larger 'freedom' movement, path of constitutionalism after independence, criticism of Congress-Indian Communists, all were directed attempt to restructure the social relations and above all knife sharpen views on several other issues from India's village system to foreign policy build up the army of both, admirers and followers as well as opponents and critics. He also levelled a fatal attack on the Communists in India for their failure to take on caste and leaving it conveniently to die its natural death with the pace of development-which has not happened at all.

The time has proved that all those charges against Dr. Ambedkar, in his liberation movement were baseless and ill-founded. There are some contradictions in struggle but all those reflect the contradictions of his time of strategies. Despite those limitations and contradictions one thing is sure and that is, Dr. Ambedkar, *"Ambedkarism"* has played a milestone role in the liberation movement and become the leading lights for millions and millions oppressed not only in India but throughout the globe.

-*-

NOTES & REFERENCES

1 Baxi Upendra, 'The Collective Conspiracy To Silence Babasaheb's Burning Thoughts', P. 61, in *Dr. Ambedkar Birth Centenary Souvenir*, Vol. IV, Ambedkar Centenary Celebration committee, England, UK, 1992.

2 Shourie Arun, *Worshipping False Gods*, ASA Publications, New Delhi, 1997.

3 For example-Riddles agitation, attack on Arun Shourie in Pune, on 26 February, 1996.

4 Dr. Ambedkar named his three Gurus-Buddha, Kabir and Mahatma Jotiba Phuley.

5 For detail discussion refer *'The Chamcha Age'*, Kanshi Ram, New Delhi, 1982.

6 Shourie Arun, *'Worshipping False Gods'*, ASA Publications, New Delhi, 1997.

7 N. M. Nimgade, 'The Thought of Dr. Babasaheb Ambedkar on Indian Agriculture' P. 70, in *Dr. Ambedkar Birth Centenary Souvenir*, Vol. III, Ambedkar Centenary Celebration committee, England, UK, 1991.

8 See-*Dr. Babasaheb Ambedkar Writings And Speeches*, Vol.1, Education Dept., Govt., of Maharashtra, 1989.

9 Jawaharlal Nehru's letter to Ambedkar, May 22, 1947, *Selected Works of Jawaharlal Nehru*, Edited by S. Gopal, II Series, Vol. II, Pp. 196-198, New Delhi, 1984.

10 *Selected Works of Jawaharlal Nehru,* Edited by S. Gopal, II Series, Vol. II, P. 196, New Delhi, 1984.

11 Presidential address of Dr. Ambedkar at Calcutta in Damodar Dam Project Conference, on 3rd January, 1945.

12 In 2007, when India completed 60th anniversary of independence we had 53% families owning less than 5 acres of land, and 1% families with more than 50 acres of land. 58% population depending on agriculture, cultivators without land are 32 million and agricultural labourers are about 100 million. Except Kerala no other State has been able to abolish fully tenancy.

13 Iyer Krishna V.R., 'Constitutionally Inscribed Social Justice and Operational Opposite Agenda in Practice', *Mainstream,* Vol. XL, No. 28, June 29, 2002, New Delhi.

14 *Constituent Assembly Debates,* Vol. VII, 22nd November, 1948, Pp. 494-495.

15 *Constituent Assembly Debates,* Vol. XII, P. 979.

16 Dr. Ambedkar address on 'Conditions Precedent For The Successful working of democracy', at District Law Library, Poona Bar, on 22nd December, 1952.

17 "Democracy is Government by Discussion".

18 "Government of the people, by the people and for the people".

19 Saturday, December 8, 1956.

20 *CAD* Vol.5, P. 788.

21 Krishna Iyer V. R., *Indian Social Justice in Crisis*, P. 26, 1983.

22 While moving the Draft Constitution in the Constituent Assembly, on 4th November, 1948.

23 For details see- Edward Luce, *In Spite of the Gods,* P. 14, ABACUS, London, 2007.

24 Ramvilas Sharma, *'Gandhi, Ambedkar, Lohia AurBhartiya Itihaski Samsyae'*, P. 540, Vani Prakashan, New Delhi, 2005.

25 Edward Luce, *In Spite of the Gods,* P. 40, ABACUS, London, 2007.

26 *Dr. Babasaheb Ambedkar Writings And Speeches*, Vol.2, P. 106, Education Dept., Govt., of Maharashtra, 1982.

27 *CAD* Book No. 2, 4th November 1948, P.62 and *Dr. Babasaheb Ambedkar Writings And Speeches*, Vol.1, Education Dept., Govt., of Maharashtra, 1994.

28 On 2oth November, 1930, in the Plenary Session of Round Table Conferences. See- *Dr. Babasaheb Ambedkar Writings And Speeches*, Vol.2, P. 55, Education Dept., Govt., of Maharashtra, 1982.

29 Resignation statement of Dr. Ambedkar, 10th October, 1951.

30 "Politics is not a game of realizing the ideal. Politics is the game of possible".

31 "Ideals are good but one must not forget that it is often dangerous to be too good".

32 *Dr. Babasaheb Ambedkar Writings And Speeches*, Vol.15, Education Dept., Govt., of Maharashtra, 1997.

33 Shourie Arun, *Worshipping False Gods*, ASA Publications, New Delhi, 1997.

34 In 1947, at Cuttack, Orissa, in a function to celebrate the foundation ceremony of Hirakud dam, Nehru made the famous statement that, such dams are the temples of modern India. But Dr. Khosla the then governor of Orissa who was present at the function said that the foundation of such temples was laid down by Dr. Ambedkar from 111942 to 1946. for details see- Sukhdeo Thorat, *'Babasaheb Ambedkar Niyojan, jal, Vidut Vikas Bhumika Yogdan'*, Sugava, Pune, 2005.

35 N.M. Nimgade, 'The Thoughts of Dr. Babasaheb Ambedkar on Indian Agriculture' P. 70, in *Dr. Ambedkar Birth Centenary Souvenir*, Vol. III, Ambedkar Centenary Celebration committee, England, UK, 1991.

36 Sukhdeo Thorat, *'Babasaheb Ambedkar Niyojan, jal, Vidut Vikas Bhumika Yogdan'*, Sugava, Pune, 2005.

37 *Dr. Babasaheb Ambedkar Writings And Speeches*, Vol.10, P. 304, Education Dept., Govt., of Maharashtra, 1991.

38 Ibid. at P. 311.

39 Ibid. at Pp. 110-111, speech delivered at the concluding session of the All India Trade Union Workers study camp held in Delhi from 8th to 17th September, 1943, under the auspices of the Indian Federation of Labour.

40 Public Speech at Mumbai, on April 26, 1942.

41 In an interview at Hyderabad, on April, 22, 1946, The Times of India, April 23, 1946.

42 *The Indian Express*, December, 2009, Mumbai.

43 Baxi Upendra, 'The Collective Conspiracy To Silence Babasaheb's Burning Thoughts', P. 64, in *Dr. Ambedkar Birth Centenary Souvenir*, Vol. IV, Ambedkar Centenary Celebration committee, England, UK, 1992.

44 Dr. Ambedkar, 'Buddha or Karl Marks', *Dr. Babasaheb Ambedkar Writings And Speeches*, Vol.14, Education Dept., Govt., of Maharashtra, 1991.

45 Gail Omvedt, 'Buddhism In India', Pp. 1-7, Sage, New Delhi, 2003.

46 D. S. Somashekhar, 'Challenges of Teaching History' in Magazine "One India One People", Pp. 20-21, June 2001.

47 Ibid.

48 Ibid.

49 Ambedkar B. R., 'Who Were The Shudras?', in *Dr. Babasaheb Ambedkar Writings And Speeches*, Vol.7, P. 16, Education Dept., Govt., of Maharashtra, 1990.

50 Ibid.

51 Ibid.

52 *Dr. Babasaheb Ambedkar Writings And Speeches*, Vol.1, P. 212, Education Dept., Govt., of Maharashtra, 1989.

53 *Constituent Assembly Debates*, Book No. 5, P. 980, Reprinted by Lok Sabha Secretariat, New Delhi, Second Reprint, 1989.

54 *Dr. Babasaheb Ambedkar Writings And Speeches*, Vol.1, Pp. 26-27, Education Dept., Govt., of Maharashtra, 1989.

55 In his Preface to Ranade, Gandhi And Jinnah, *Dr. Babasaheb Ambedkar Writings And Speeches*, Vol.1, P. 209, Education Dept., Govt., of Maharashtra, 1989.

56 *Dr. Babasaheb Ambedkar Writings And Speeches*, Vol.1, Pp. 47, 41, Education Dept., Govt., of Maharashtra, 1989.

57 *Dr. Babasaheb Ambedkar Writings And Speeches*, Vol.1, Education Dept., Govt., of Maharashtra, 1989.

-*-